forgotten places

forgotten places

the holocaust
and the remnants of destruction
a photographic essay

Photographs and text by Stephen D. Smith

Published by

Quill

in conjunction with
Beth Shalom Holocaust Memorial Centre

in memory

of the

forgotten

forgotten places

the holocaust
and the remnants of destruction
a photographic essay

Stephen D. Smith

Published in 2000 in Great Britain by
Quill Press,
P.O.BOX 2002,
Newark,
Nottinghamshire,
NG22 9ZG.

British Library Cataloguing in Publication Data
A Catalogue reference for this book is available from the
British Library

ISBN: 0 953 62802 7

Graphic Design: CDA Creative Communications

Printed and Bound by: Polestar Wheatons Ltd.

introduction

'Every picture tells a story...' Or so it is said.

This is a book of photographs about the Holocaust. It does not contain images of the Holocaust, but of that which remains. It is a memorial in its own right. It is also about memorials and how we interpret them. The pictures are what I have seen, or at least what I chose to see, as I took groups of people to discover something of the tragedy of the Holocaust in Poland. They are images which have been composed and selected to tell a story. They are honest - as the camera never lies - but they have been chosen for their meaning to me. The result is a photographic essay, a reflection on the remnants of destruction of European Jews.

Some of the pictures are tragic, some are lonely, some are provocative, others enraging. All were taken with one purpose; to demonstrate that all too often our understanding of what and who was lost is limited by the symbols we use to represent them. I am aware, too, that this interpretation is my own and may be one of many different ways of looking at the same places.

By necessity the scope of this publication is limited. Firstly it is limited by the choice of country. It is true that almost half of the victims of the Holocaust were Polish Jews and that the Nazis chose to place their most infamous sites of destruction on Polish soil. But the Nazis left their legacy of destruction wherever they went. A more substantial analysis would, and perhaps should, focus on a number of countries and experiences. The essay is also limited by the sites I have

forgotten
places
the holocaust
and the remnants of destruction

chosen to study. There are hundreds of sites of mass murder in Poland alone. Every city, every town and virtually every village had its Jewish population. Each could be a study in its own right, as each experienced the fear, the turmoil and the loss of mass murder. Each in its own way is a place of memorial to its victims. That said, it is hoped these limitations enhance the focus, and hence serve as an illustration of the issues as a whole.

It is important for me to clarify further the style and approach of this publication. I understand that this is a creative publication about an ugly topic. The care which has gone into producing this publication simply reflects the way I feel about the importance of the Holocaust. The same care could have gone into producing something stark and grey, but that is not how I see things through the lens. The Holocaust was and is in colour. Secondly, this book is intended to be a memorial in its own way. The inherent danger is that in questioning the symbols and images we use, new ones could inadvertently be created. I want it to be understood that the images I have chosen to take are only a small part of a very large mosaic one could create. It is also important to note that I have chosen not to photograph nor to publish images of some of the places which have the deepest personal meaning to me. I have not included many photographs of Belzec and only briefly focused on Majdanek, Treblinka and Chelmno. This is not because I do not find them touching, but precisely because I do.

I have chosen to divide the book into three sections. The first part is a short essay, outlining some of the theory behind memorialisation and the collective memory of the Holocaust. It attempts to outline some of the pitfalls of memory; why it is we create symbols to assist our comprehension, and how we must set about criticising those symbols.

The photographic collection is divided into two sections. The first, 'Shadows of a Former World', looks at the remnants of a past Jewish life. Most of the photographs were taken in and around Krakow and Tarnow in southern Poland. The second section of photographic images, 'Where Memories Meet', examines the sites of mass destruction in Poland, and particularly focuses on the camps of Auschwitz and Birkenau. This choice is deliberate, as there are already a substantial number of images and symbols focused around the camps at the Auschwitz complex, not to mention the controversy which surfaces with disturbing regularity. These images will hopefully serve to challenge some of the symbols currently in circulation, and ask how images can enhance our critical faculties, rather than limiting our interpretation of historical events.

Most of all, these photographs are about who was lost and how we remember them, and how we must learn to understand the ever fainter shadows of their memory.

forgotten places

Mass Grave: Zbylitowksa Gora

I was standing in a small woodland tucked away behind an insignificant Polish village named Zbylitowska Gora. Staring blankly at the rolling leafy undergrowth, I wandered around under the tall trees which had silently stood there looking on for many decades. There was nothing particularly unusual about this small patch of forest, except that here, in June 1942, some six thousand Jews were marched out of the Tarnow ghetto, a short five kilometre walk away, and were shot dead. Among them were no less than eight hundred children. As I stood there, gazing at the grey rickety fences which marked the mass grave containing the remains of those innocent lives, I realised something afresh; or maybe it just hit me for the first time. The Nazi regime had not only orchestrated the untimely and brutal murders of these children, but also the complete and intentional erasure of their innocent lives from all memory. And, what is more, by and large it was successful. Nobody knew who was buried at Zbylitowska Gora, and nobody really cared. I found myself staring the real horror of the Holocaust straight in the face: for try as I might to bring them back, the memory of those eight hundred children is forever lost. They will never be, not even in death, the individuals they were born to be. They inhabit the forgotten places of the Holocaust.

the memory of those eight hundred children is forever lost

In confronting these forgotten places, we encounter the necessity of remembering the Holocaust and the difficulty of so doing. Difficult, not because we do not wish to remember, but because the incomprehensible scale of the terror and the absence it leaves, almost defies us to remember it. What can be remembered sufficiently about something so dark, so hidden, so absolute? We should also address how we use symbols to help us answer those questions and assist us in our representation. There is little doubt that the Holocaust *is* symbolic and it is inevitable that, with time, we will develop symbols to help us explain it both to ourselves and to others. But the type of symbols we use, and why, still require further thought, reflection and understanding.

Behind this comment lies a concern. A concern that we all - myself included - with the very best intentions, console ourselves in the light of the Holocaust by prompting ourselves to remember. What we do not always make as clear is, what we want to remember, whom we want to remember, and precisely why. The call to 'remember' has long since become a cliché. Then with the best of intentions the events of the Holocaust, and worse, the victims themselves, are reduced to no more than a symbolic gesture of anonymous remembrance.

It appears that we often hope the commitment to remember, itself, will suffice. The result is the emergence of the imperative: 'Remember!' - often heard in its Hebrew variant *'Zachor!'* - which generally comes without clarification, and certainly does not contain a self-apparent definition of what and who is to be remembered. The fear is that, should we not develop a clear knowledge of what or who we want to remember, the Holocaust will become either a black hole somewhere in our historical conscience, without meaning, explanation or form, or simply be reduced to a symbol. Then, despite our best efforts, we will actually forget more, far more, than we can ever hope to remember.

When we say *'Zachor!'*, it seems we encourage all to become witnesses, without distinction. This is achieved within society by creating vehicles of remembrance, such as a documentary film, a memorial monument, literature, or commemorations. By way of illustration, when in January 1995 the BBC ran a series of programmes on the Holocaust to commemorate the fiftieth anniversary of the liberation of Auschwitz, they called it the 'Remember' season. The programmes themselves were mainly historical documentaries; but what accompanied the factual information imparted to the general public was the assumed imperative for society to 'Remember'.

Deep in thought: Kate at Auschwitz-Birkenau

Memorialising events is not so simple. On 27 January that same year, thousands of people stood at the end of the so-called 'ramp' at Birkenau. The occasion was the fiftieth anniversary of the liberation of the camp by the Soviets. What was clear among the sea of faces gathered there, is that they were all there for very different reasons. Some were survivors, some were families, some were clergy, some were heads of state, many were journalists, some were Jewish; interestingly, most were not. However, to each, 'Auschwitz' was a symbol, a place wherein their desire to remember, at whatever level and for whatever reason, could be carried out. Disappointingly, few would probably agree on exactly what and who should be remembered there, except in vague generalities. 'Auschwitz' therefore means different things to different people. Jonathan Webber's concept of a 'multiplicity of memories' at Auschwitz[1] was clearly evidenced there that day, and continues to be today.

There is a reason, of course. 'Auschwitz' *does* mean different things to different people, because a variety of groups and individuals suffered a spectrum of tragic circumstances there. Auschwitz, as a concentration camp used for the incarceration of the Polish intelligentsia and political opponents of the Nazis, was established and infamous before the first Jews were taken there under the terms of the 'Final Solution'. For Poles that infamy remains, independent of the mass destruction of European Jewry. For the Jewish world, the focus of Auschwitz is ever more intense as large numbers of survivors testify to the mass murder of Jews from right across the European continent. Actually, what many fail to understand is that while Auschwitz may contain multiple memories, Auschwitz was also many places. It is true that the forty-four camps were administered as a unit, but each had its own identity, its own regime and its own set of outcomes. Birkenau was *not* Auschwitz I, any more than Buna-Monowitz was Birkenau. Each needs to be seen and understood separately because their symbolism and hence their meaning is contained in their differing histories.

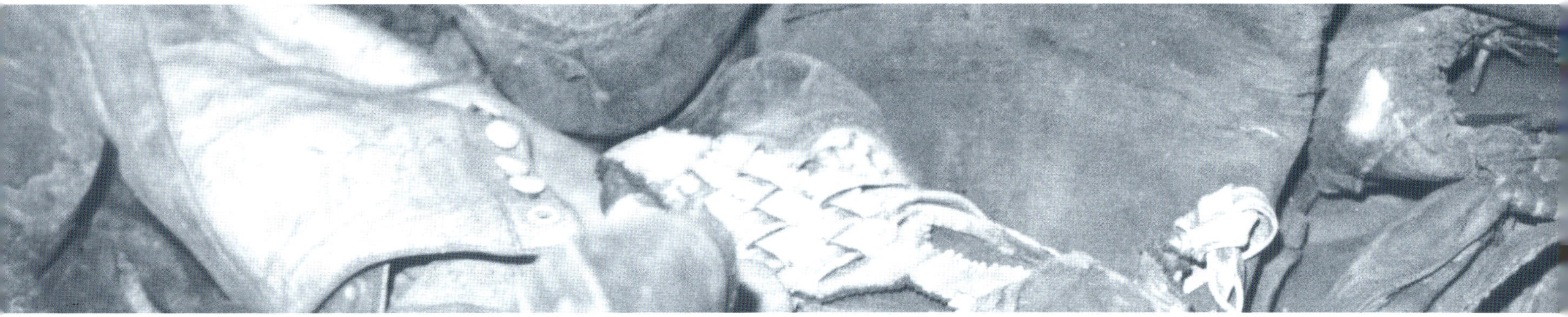

Shoes: Majdanek

1 Jonathan Webber. *The Future of Auschwitz: Some Personal Reflections*. Oxford: The Oxford Centre for Post-Graduate Hebrew Studies, Frank Green Lecture Number One, 1992.

For the Polish people, Auschwitz represents the 'martyrdom' of the Poles under the Nazis. That is their understanding because that was a part of their experience there. Had Auschwitz I existed without Birkenau, it is doubtful it would dominate our memory more than similar sites of tragedy such as Dachau or Mauthausen. For the Poles, however, little would change. It is the presence of Birkenau which makes the reality of 'Auschwitz' so dreaded for Jews and it is the existence of Auschwitz I which makes 'Oswieçim' such a place of infamy for the Poles. The lack of mutual understanding on this distinction causes the clash of memory that so often exists there.

One thing becomes clear; we shape memory, as much as it shapes us. We tell ourselves what we want to remember, about what, about whom, and how. Subsequent events, political developments and present societal circumstances shape this memory. There is a specific problem with the memory of the Holocaust, however. Memory only has meaning when linked to experiences that are communicable. It seems the experience of the Holocaust evades even the rich and complex textures of language itself. How do you represent something so difficult to communicate? How do you describe such horrific events and hope that your reader or listener understands, or interprets them in a meaningful way?

Mezuzah: Tarnow

In 1986 Claude Lanzmann launched his seminal film on the Holocaust. Entitled *Shoah*, the nine and a half hour documentary comprised mainly the voices of the victims of Nazi death camps recounting their grim experiences. One of the survivors, a Michael Podchlebnik, describes his own experience at Chelmno in which he had to bury his own family in a mass grave. He states that he too died at Chelmno. During this harrowing episode, he states through his interpreter:

"But he's only human, and he wants to live. So he must forget. He thanks God for what remains, and that he can forget. And let's not talk about that."

Podchlebnik may not have expressed the desire to talk about *'that'*, because of the impossibility of so doing, but also because it was a part of his own personal history.[2] *'That'* to him was a part of him, it needed no further explanation for him to understand it. Before we can fulfil our role in remembrance, we too have to know something of the historical context and to make 'that' meaningful in a personal way.

In developing an understanding of the Holocaust, we somehow have to begin with the very contemporaneous nature of it. We identify the Holocaust as being history, but the Holocaust did not happen in the dim and distant past. It is still contemporary, persisting as a never-ending nightmare in the hearts and minds of the survivors - its victims still today. What we tend to forget, or at least talk of less, is that there are also perpetrators, collaborators and sympathisers in even greater numbers. These individuals are also a contemporary reminder that we, those of us still participating in society today, committed these crimes - and suffered the loss.

The past will remain a part of the present for only a short time. The more distant it becomes, the more we feel the need to keep it present and the more we therefore represent it. And representation is problematic. As soon as we start to interpret, to represent and to analyse, it becomes more and more fixed. Then we either limit it or sensationalise it. By placing distance between ourselves and events, we can inadvertently remove responsibility from the present. If it happened there and then, it can start to have less relevance for the here and now. Our historical analysis can inadvertently distance us from the very problem we are attempting to deal with, and hence no longer make us feel the need to. The writing of history must therefore involve us in

2 David Carrol in: Lyotard, Jean François. *Heidegger and 'the jews'*. Trans. Andréas Michel, and Mark Roberts. Minneapolis: University of Minnesota Press, 1990. p viii.

Generations: Nathan in his old school, Bendzin

some way. It must attempt to write the Holocaust into the present, not remove it to the historiographical dustbin of the past.

This does not refer only to the writing of history. In our memorial culture, the Holocaust has become a part of the world in which we live. We need to constantly assess why we are interested in making its profile more prominent. Hopefully our motives are not simply to sensationalise or make public someone else's suffering. The reality is, the Holocaust does have a presence within our contemporary conscience and rightly so, but how we communicate that to future generations requires careful and considered thought.

Considering the development of attention being given to remembrance of the Holocaust currently, Lawrence Langer postulates that: 'Perhaps...we have begun to enter the second stage of Holocaust response, moving from what we know of the event (the province of historians), to how to remember it, which shifts the responsibility to our own imaginations and what we are prepared to admit there.'[3] It might also be suggested that the next step in this process is the movement from remembrance to education; the means by which society appropriates the past as a part of the present. It is necessary to develop an understanding of memory at both the individual and societal level and to have the constructs within society to deal with the necessity to remember.

Jean François Lyotard writes about 'the politics of forgetting', in which memorialisation performs the function of limitation.[4] In this case remembrance of the Holocaust could be as much about providing a short-term salve, as about healing the wounds of the past. To make this more complex, the problem facing any individual or community is the inherently incomprehensible nature of the Holocaust experience. Naturally, this leads to reconstruction, revision or limitation; even with the very best of intentions. Before beginning to construct a methodology capable of observing and defining an approach to Holocaust remembrance, the complex nature of the events themselves must first be addressed.

In the same way, Geoffrey Hartman observes the difficulty of finding what he describes as a guiding image from the 'black sun' of the destruction of the Jews. He comments that it 'produces a melancholy as disabling as anything ever known.'[5] This melancholy is like a shadow cast over the endeavours of witness, which serves both as its motivation and its major hindrance. The witness seeks to explain the meaning of the Holocaust, but is simultaneously subsumed by the impossibility of so doing. Theodore Adorno is often quoted for his now famous dictum that 'to write poetry after Auschwitz is barbaric',[6] emphasising the difficulty of any representation of such events.[7] Scholars the world over have struggled with the way in which we interpret these events and we remain acutely aware of the difficulties we face. Commenting on the difficulty of telling, Elie Wiesel postulates that perhaps silence would have been the best way for the survivors to have explained the impossibility of telling their stories.[8] Wiesel, through his prolific writing on his experiences of the Holocaust, has chosen speech in preference to silence. Historian Michael Marrus stated that had Wiesel chosen silence, it would have been a 'counsel of despair - leading to falsification or to oblivion'.[9] However, even the professional historian approaches the history of the Holocaust with a sense of unease. Marrus argues in favour of documenting this history as history, but simultaneously recognises the sense of limitation in discussing conditions 'so utterly outside our experience'.[10] Lyotard similarly

3 Lawrence Langer. *Admitting the Holocaust.* Oxford: Oxford U.P. 1995.
4 Jean François Lyotard. *Heidegger and 'the jews'.* Trans. Andreas Michel and Mark Roberts. Minneapolis: University of Minnesota Press, 1990. p.7.
5 Geoffrey Hartman. *Holocaust Remembrance. The Shapes of Memory.* Oxford: Blackwell, 1994. p.2.
6 Theodore Adorno. "Culture Criticism and Society", in *Prisms*, trans. Samuel and Shierry Weber. London: Neville Spearman, 1967. p.34.
7 Sidra DeKoven Ezrahi expressing concern that this dictum has been taken as Adorno's final word on the matter further elucidates his position pointing out that he made many visits to Auschwitz. He qualifies his previous statement saying; "the abundance of real suffering tolerates no forgetting...this suffering demands the continued existence of art [even as]...it prohibits it. It is now virtually in art alone that suffering can find its own voice." Quoted by Sidra DeKoven Ezrahi, "Graves in the Air" in Saul Friedlander, *Probing the Limits of Representation: Nazism and the Final Solution*, Cambridge Mass and London: Harvard U.P. 1992. p.260.
8 Elie Wiesel. *One Generation After.* New York: Schocken Books, 1982. p.10.
9 Michael Marrus. *The Holocaust in History*. London: Penguin, 1987. p.7.
10 ibid. p 6.

recognises the limitations of the writing of history and rejects the possibility that history as a science can address the realism of the situation concerned.[11] He also advocates the learning of history as part of the fight against forgetting, as forgetting involves the limitation of what people wish to know.

What our learning of history demonstrates is the often incomprehensible nature of an unprecedented and unparalleled set of events. This has led commentators to describe the Holocaust with new terminology. Descriptive titles such as 'caesura', 'the tremendum', 'planet Auschwitz' and more commonly-used terms such as *'Shoah'* and 'Holocaust' all present an event beyond normal terms of reference. Each attempts to illuminate something of the impossibility of knowing anything fully. Because as the role of the witness is to illuminate and expose, the nature of the events are such that they obfuscate knowledge and witness.

The call to 'remember!' within the Jewish community is perhaps best understood as a call for a 'community of memory', in which all within the community work together to construct meaning out of the Holocaust, which no one person could achieve independently.[12] But this is not an experience limited to the Jewish world. As an issue for humanity, the emergence of a community of memory becomes a human duty or at least an imperative for anyone to answer. If remembrance is the specific and unavoidable duty of the Jewish community, it should be a common duty for those who so volunteer to witness the tragedy of their fellow human beings.

The development of a 'community of memory' of the Holocaust is not only bound in with events of the past, but grapples with their representation in the present. But our forms of representation all encounter boundaries. Monuments are limited by their form and by interpretation. Metaphoric remembrance, as found most commonly in literature, presents similar strictures as a metaphor is only as powerful as the reader's ability, or desire, to interpret it. If we remain silent we might never know. If we represent, we may either numb our senses with

The Great *Shul*: Nathan and his wife Jill where once stood the Synagogue, Bendzin

the horror of it, or create a norm out of the entirely abnormal.

This can be clearly demonstrated by the way in which survivors give testimony and how we struggle to interpret them. The problem lies in the ability of survivors to speak sufficiently about the unspeakable and the ability of the hearer to make sense of events beyond their own experience. Jean François Lyotard says that 'Holocaust art does not say the unsayable, but says that it cannot say it',[13] but Lawrence Langer doubts that the same can be said of Holocaust testimony. This is not because of what the survivors say, but the way in which they are interpreted. On hearing the testimony, as impossible as it is to understand, the hearer translates the events into comprehensible possibilities. The witness and the witness's witness then become a communal 'we', translating the victims' experience into shared experience of history. Langer comments that such referents convert death in the gas chamber into a norm, acceptable to the generations that have to live with the memory of this atrocity.[14]

11 Lyotard. *Heidegger and...* op cit. p.9
12 Hutchins, 1988, in David Middleton and Derek Edwards, eds. *Collective Remembering.* London: Sage Publications, 1990. p.8.
13 Lyotard, *Heidegger and...* op cit. p.47.
14 Langer, *Admitting...* op cit. p.20.

This is how symbols emerge. Through symbols our representation becomes more communicable and many of the difficult nuances of meaning and interpretation are circumvented. We create a symbol to deal with the general meaning and in some manner avoid the detail. The rules seem to be that if you do not know how to say it, symbolise it; if you do not understand it, symbolise it; if you have a message to get out of it, symbolise it. The symbols then replace the events in part and actually become the memory. It is not that use of symbols is problematic in itself, but many of the symbols we use are. This is why we need to examine the symbols we use, or at least ask why they are there.

To further evaluate this line of enquiry we might go back to the symbol of 'Auschwitz' for a moment more. The reason 'Auschwitz' has become such a potent and indeed important symbol, is because people lived there, as well as died there. People survived to tell the story - usually the story of their survival. While undoubtedly it is a powerful symbol, it cannot convey the entirety of the Holocaust itself, as more inmates survived 'Auschwitz' than any of the other death camps. I do not wish to confuse here, as this was largely due to the large numbers of people transported and distributed from there. One million two hundred thousand Jews murdered at Birkenau is indeed hugely and tragically significant, but it represents less than one quarter of the six million or so victims. Are the other four million eight hundred thousand less significant, or is it that we are starting to make 'Auschwitz' a convenient symbol to summarise that which we do not know or understand or, dare I say it, do not really care about?

This confusion can also be illustrated by a number of incidents surrounding the present Auschwitz museum complex, where Catholic responses have been, at best, muddled. As we have discussed, Auschwitz is also an important symbol to the Polish people. Polish Catholics reflect on it as the place of Polish martyrdom under the Nazis, which has its own validity, but in a different way to the mass murder of Europe's Jews there. A 'Jewish Pavilion' containing an historical exhibit of the Jewish experience in the Holocaust was established in one of the blocks at Auschwitz I. But following fresh waves of antisemitism in 1967, the pavilion was closed following the Six Day War. It was not reopened until 1978, when it was rededicated by President Chaim Herzog of Israel. James Young highlights the confusion still apparent then, citing Polish minister of culture Janusz Wieczorek as saying at the rededication:

'Among the doomed, Jews and Poles rank in the first place...Oswieçim, Treblinka, Chelmno, Plasow, Belzec, Sobibor, Lodz, Bialystok, and the Warsaw Ghetto and dozens of other places of 'the Warta district' and 'the General Gubernyia' - they are all stages of extermination, stations of the Cross of Polish Jews...we know nearly everything about their gehenna [Calvary] (sic), the misery of the Poles.'

This metaphorical representation of Auschwitz as the Calvary, or hell, of the Polish Jews is perhaps due to an ignorance of the meaning of both Auschwitz, Calvary and hell to Jews. However, his equation with Jews and Poles serves only as an insult to the Jews who were subjected to treatment more severe and ultimately more absolute in its consequences than any form of comparison would justify. The competition for a more

If we remain silent we might never know. If we represent, we may either numb our senses with the horror of it all, or create a norm out of the entirely abnormal.

complete suffering, in a comparative memory of Auschwitz, serves to further intensify the clear misappropriation of the memory of it. The metaphor of Auschwitz as a 'Golgotha of the contemporary world' was further endorsed by Pope John Paul II on a visit to the complex in 1979, when he also expressed the Holocaust as being 'the martyrdom of Christ recapitulated in the mass murder of the Jews'.

The creation of such symbolism not only distorts, but confuses an audience seeking understanding and rewrites history to suit a short-term political objective. At times we all do it, intentionally or not. When the symbolism we create occludes the meaning and tragedy of the individual, they too become forgotten places of the Holocaust experience. Through the pictures that follow we will explore some of these forgotten places, as it is only when we know the danger of our varied forms of 'forgetting' that we learn the importance of the forms of remembrance we adopt.

Recently, I was at the site of the Belzec death camp in south-eastern Poland. Unlike the Auschwitz museum today, with its cafeterias and smiling guides, Belzec is a deserted, unkempt patch of ground next to a woodyard just off the freight line which runs north-south along the main road. You have to make a special journey there. There is nothing to see there. The chain-link fence, which roughly demarcates where it is thought the camp was, is not maintained. The ugly, soon to be replaced, grey concrete memorial amongst the trees simply declares itself to be there 'In memory of the victims of the Hitlerite terror'. I struggled through some twelve inches of snow to make my way across the camp just to see how large, or small, the territory was. Nobody had been there in over two weeks. The snow, which had lain for some considerable time, did not have so much as a footprint in it.

In excess of six hundred thousand Jews were murdered on that small piece of scrub land, most of them before Birkenau saw its first transports of mass death. Several thousand people were murdered there each day. In the Jewish tradition there would be several thousand *yahrzeits* there every day, and no one had even *been* there for over two weeks. Where are the candles? Where are the prayers? Where is the memory? In truth, the majority of the victims have no memorial, as there is no one to remember them. Half the number of people were murdered in a camp which would have fitted into Birkenau many times over. I stood there bemused by this sight. I understood nothing.

I left Belzec and made my way to Krakow, with a slight detour, making a brief stop at Nowy Sacz. There is little to see of the old Jewish life in this once vibrant community. The synagogue in the town square is now a museum and of course there is the cemetery. It was late in the day when we entered the cemetery, but in the fading winter light a *yahrzeit* lamp was flickering brightly in the *ohel* of one of the Halberstam dynasty at the cemetery. I looked at the glow of the candle, wondering what *hasid* had travelled to light it. Had he or she come specially? From Jerusalem or New York? Then my mind switched back to Belzec, and I realised that I was yet to visit the *ohel* of a great *tzaddik* buried in Poland, where someone had not been recently, said their prayers, lit their candles, then gone their way. I had visited Gora Kalwaria, Kock and Bobowa and at each the memory of the great and the wise was being upheld with some sense of dignity.

But what of the six hundred thousand souls, some great, some wise, some neither;

The site of the former death camp at Belzec

buried, scattered...lost at Belzec? The reason the *tzaddik* is remembered is because his life and teaching is appreciated. The *hasid* returns to the resting place of the *tzaddik* because he has survivors who will bear witness to the greatness of his teaching and will continue to uphold it, even after his death. The *hasid is* the memory of the *tzaddik*, so long as he is prepared to travel halfway around the world, to say *kaddish* and light his lamp. The moment he ceases to go, the moment he ceases to remember and appreciate, the *tzaddik* is no more.

Hitler intended to wipe out European Jewry without trace. Still his intent can succeed in obfuscating that civilisation, unless like the *hasid*, we make it our duty not just to say we will remember, but when necessary, to travel halfway around the world to light a single candle for a single man, woman or child.

That duty is not only the duty of Jews but of anyone who cares about the suffering of the Jews and of humanity. The Holocaust should not lead to exclusivity, but to further inclusive understanding. Put simply, we should learn to share experiences, pain and remembrance with each other, whoever we are.

Still today, survivors of the Holocaust write, talk, share and carry out their terrible mission of bearing witness to the destruction of the European Jews. By their actions, the memory of those communities lives on. Soon, the survivor community will no longer be able to perform that function. *We* will be the bearers of witness. At that moment, cliché and roughshod symbolism will be an insult to the true witnesses whose blood continues to cry out from the stained earth of Europe. Then, the eight hundred children of Zbylitowska Gora and the six hundred thousand victims of Belzec and over five million other victims will only have us.

We not only have a responsibility to take our duty to remember seriously.

We are their memory.

Lighting a candle in memory of the dead: Birkenau

shadows

of a former world

Close-up of a *matzevah* in the Remuh cemetery, Kazimierz, Krakow.

ruins

Matzevah in Autumn, Jewish Cemetery, Krakow.

Not everything is lost if its memory still lingers in my heart

Fichman

# of a forgotten world

The dead are the only sign of life. That is the way it is here.

Large cemeteries, beautiful cemeteries, broken cemeteries, lost cemeteries; if you want to discover anything about the communities of Poland destroyed by the Nazis, all that are left are the fading and dishevelled headstones of a once vibrant world. Today, they are the key to commemoration, the vehicle of memory. The names, inscribed on a million and more overgrown *matzevot*, are the people who lived here and died here. They lived in peace and died in peace. Or at least they lived out their lives in the place where they were born. They worked and prayed and made ends meet; now in favour, now being hounded by the mob. When they were done, their brethren gave them an honourable burial. Their souls, of blessed memory, were part of a world within a world. Perhaps they loved it, maybe they despised it, but they were a part of it. They are the absence we feel.

Inscribed in stone are the names and the deeds of these communities. They are our link to a time now gone. But they too dwell in obscurity. Save for the few pilgrims who come their way, largely they lie unappreciated and unkempt. Who really cares today about the communities that once lived here? Who has the time or resources to repair, restore and memorialise them? And toward what end? They can never be brought back. Or can they?

Preservation is a duty. If not, the dim light of their passing will surely fade forever.

life among the dead

as in life,
so in death.

The presence of life was somehow symbolised in this iris growing in the Remuh cemetery at Kazimierz, Krakow; its singular beauty like a *matzevah* in its own right.

As in life, so in death.

Like cemeteries the world over, scoundrels lie with the pious, the rich with the poor, the scholar with the imbecile. So, too, the famous and the obscure mingle among the *matzevot*. It is a lost world, a civilisation which will never be recreated. And this is as close as you come.

Beauty, history and most of all individuality I find here. Names, like glimpses through an otherwise locked window, give a momentary view into an otherwise unknown world. Each name is an individual. In life they were representatives of a community, of a family and of the historical events in which they participated. And so they remain in death. Not everyone was famous of course; but everyone did have a name. The anonymity of the Holocaust is in part the overwhelming oblivion we feel. But these names - the names of their ancestors - preserve their families' identities *in absentia*. We know the victims, if only in part, by their forebears.

These then are places of the perpetuation of memory. To preserve them is not to become lost in the futility of nostalgic longing, but to respect them and to breathe life back into their otherwise obliterated history. Their achievements, their struggle, their good times and their bad times are part of the make-up of the European Jewish experience. To know them is to overcome the utter absence that the 'Final Solution' attempted to achieve. The Nazis attempted to wipe out the Jews of Europe and intended to obscure their memory. To honour the history of these communities is to defeat that still achievable attempt to impose the evil of forgetfulness.

What caught my eye here was the prominently displayed name - Drezner. I do not know who this individual was, but the clear inscription of this family name indicates the power of individual memory.

Matzevah in the Hasidic centre of Kock, near Warsaw. The sparse placing of the *matzevot* is typical of many cemeteries plundered by local inhabitants. This one has been re-erected with a new concrete base.

Memory sustains man in the world of life.

S. D. Luzzatto

Here
in a small way,
sometimes,
but only sometimes, the
threads
can be connected.

The family of Kitty-Hart Moxon were once known to be buried in Andrychow. In our search for names, eventually the names of her mother's family - Felix - started to emerge from among the brambles. Some she never knew and had never heard of. Some names simply had virtues and vices attached to their memory. But just to know that they were there and undisturbed was important.

in search of the forgotten

Forgetfulness prolongs the exile, memory is the key to redemption.

Baal Shem Tov

This is not about rooting around in graveyards. It is about rediscovering the past.

Like taking pieces of a jigsaw and slowly, tediously building a picture, until the fragments start to make sense as a whole. Finding the meaning of each of these starts to paint an ever more vivid image. Sadly, never will a full picture be possible.

Among the thousands of *matzevot* lie buried the names of families of those who survived and then moved on, or those who could never come back. Tragically, these family graves are often lost forever. Occasionally they are there: a mother, an aunt, a cousin, or a whole family of names. People who are not necessarily known, but known to be part of the family.

Searching among the *matzevot* is also about finding people's identity; people who otherwise might never know entirely who they are, or to whom they are connected. The dark shadow of the Holocaust prevented many families knowing their roots, or even venturing to look. Here in a small way, sometimes, but only sometimes, the threads can be connected.

Looking through the undergrowth is at times frustrating, particularly as it is unclear whether one will ever find anything meaningful. But the importance of knowing can never really be overstated. If the key to comprehending the immense tragedy of the Holocaust is understanding the communities that were lost, then finding them and naming them should surely bring us closer to them.

The *matzevah* of one of Kitty's relatives, Adolf Felix.

In Bielsko, the neatly trimmed lawns at the entry to the cemetery belied a disappointing history. Many *matzevot* were missing, including those of Kitty's family buried there.

We found many *matzevot* of the Felix family, testament to their presence and involvement in the Andrychow community.

kvetl'ch wishes

Rabbi Moses Isserles, known as Remuh, one of the great Rabbis of Krakow, lies buried in the cemetery named after him - the Remuh cemetery in Kazimierz. Here the pious come to offer supplication and his grave is distinguished by the large number of *kvetl'ch* left by pilgrims.

A Hasidic pilgrim visits the *matzevot* of *tzaddikim* in the Warsaw Jewish cemetery.

It is a *mitzvah* to go and pray at the graves of the righteous. To leave a *kvetl'ch* - a wish or a prayer - is opportunity to have your prayer heard, as the Almighty will surely look favourably on prayers offered at the graves of the learned and good.

Today, Hasidim still travel from all over the world on the *yahrzeit* of the death of a great *tzaddik* - a righteous man - to say *kaddish* at his *ohel*, to light a candle and to leave a *kvetl'ch*. Their fleeting presence and the signs they leave behind are evidence of the legacy of these teachers' influence. The communities they spawned in Poland no longer exist, but their descendants and followers leave their New York or Jerusalem apartments to travel to the home of their spiritual roots to remember and to pray.

And so the tradition lives on.

With God there is no forgetting.

Talmud Yerushalmi, Yoma

Millions of souls could not be, and indeed were not, murdered in absolute secrecy.

There were many witnesses to the destruction of European Jewry. What was said and done at the time, history has now proven, was too little. It is true that the force of the Nazi onslaught was overwhelming and that the oppression visited upon occupied populations was very great. However, as your neighbours and friends are led away to be slaughtered, to remain silent seems a heavy responsibility to assume.

And yet there were many who did just that.

Was it ignorance or belligerence? Was it fear or self-preservation? The answer is probably 'yes', all of that and more. But now, as you stand in the deserted streets and search out the hidden vestiges of the lives of those destroyed, one wonders how such destruction could ever have been desirable for anyone to see, to hear and then to ignore. As if it does not matter.

It is springtime and the trees are coming into leaf. The greens of spring pushing through the decaying browns of autumn. Conkers lie on the ground, testimony to the cycle of life, death and rebirth which continues here.

Conkers litter the floor of the cemetery.

On the edge of a mass grave in the Jewish Cemetery of Tarnow, a tree comes into bud once more. Some six thousand murdered Jews are buried here, and this tree, like many living in the environs, remains a silent witness. It saw everything and heard everything, and says nothing. And so the ebb and flow of summer and winter, life and death, continue.

But not for the Jews.

Jews just die here.

The *matzevah* of Abraham Ladner, the last Jew of Tarnow.

Chestnut tree coming into bud, Tarnow Jewish Cemetery. It was the concept of re-birth which really troubled me as I looked at this scene. The chestnut tree was simply following its cycle of regeneration uninterrupted, yet everything seemed to be at a standstill in the cemetery.

the silent witness

the desecration of memory.

Mass grave: This broken column from the destroyed Great Synagogue indicates the place where some six thousand Jews of Tarnow were buried in a mass grave. Today its proximity to the town is telling. From the high-rise buildings in the suburbs of town, people carry on with their lives.

Not everyone respects these places of memory.

For the majority of people living around them, they are no more than decaying relics of the past. 'The Jews were a bad thing anyway, so better they are gone' is often the unspoken subtext of their attitude. Headstones are taken or desecrated, cemetery property damaged and in many instances cemeteries turn into parks, scrubland or are even designated for development.

Not everyone has the privilege of a dignified death, but there is an obligation on those who remain to maintain a dignified place of memorial. Cemeteries should be places of respect and blessed memory.

Ghetto fields: In the Lodz ghetto, individuals who died were at least afforded the dignity of an individual burial. Over sixty thousand corpses were buried in what is now known as the ghetto fields in the Lodz Jewish cemetery. Some do have headstones, many do not, but amazingly the identity of the majority has been preserved by the community, even in the face of mass death.

Every soul should be laid to rest in peace, if not decorum. Sadly, this does not always remain so.

During the Nazi occupation, Jewish cemeteries were often turned into killing grounds where mass executions were carried out, or the corpses of the deceased were buried *en masse*. Apart from the tragedy itself, everything that happened was in direct contravention of Jewish laws and ethics.

To be places of memory, they must also be places of dignity, if only to overcome the indignity they have been afforded for too long.

The latter troubles
make us forget the first.

Talmud Berakhot

Pogrom: In Kielce, as in other Polish towns after the conclusion of the war, Jews returned home to an unfriendly welcome. Forty-six Jews were killed in Kielce. Their memorial now stands in what remains of the Jewish cemetery.

Some of these cemeteries hold secrets which need to be told.

Desecration: The dismembered *matzevah* of Stefanja Wilczynska, assistant to Janusz Korczak in his ghetto orphanage.

In the sewers: A manhole to the Warsaw sewage network in the Warsaw Jewish Cemetery. Effluent still thunders through the channels once used by smugglers and resisters to navigate the territory above.

Hevrah Kaddishe: The *matzevah* of Eliasz Pinkis, one of the family who were members of the *Hevrah Kaddishe*, the burial society, in the Warsaw ghetto.

# of heroes and martyrs

Man cannot die twice or escape from dying once.

Mishlé Yoav

Some of these cemeteries hold secrets which need to be told.

Buried here are some of the men and women who lived through the Holocaust. Some survived; others did not. To find and to tell their stories is to remember them where they lived and died.

There are many examples. For instance, Adam Czerniakow, head of the *Judenrat* in the Warsaw ghetto, is buried in the Warsaw Jewish cemetery. He committed suicide when ordered by the Nazis to provide six thousand people a day from the ghetto for 'resettlement'. After the war, the survivors of the community erected his *matzevah*.

Janusz Korczak was murdered in Treblinka, but has a monument in the Warsaw cemetery in memory of the fine example he set in caring for the children of his orphanage until their untimely deaths. The children of the ghetto whom he cared for are seen trailing behind him as they prepare for the transport to Treblinka. Korczak's assistant Stafania Wielczynska also has a *matzevah* in the cemetery. A few days before I was here, vandals tried to remove it. Now it lies in ruins.

Perhaps more obscure *matzevot* in the Warsaw cemetery are those of the Pinkis family who were members of the *hevrah kaddishe* in the ghetto. Daily, they and others would walk around the streets of the ghetto collecting bodies thrown onto the sidewalks. They would take them to the cemetery and bury them there. Many were simply buried in mass graves as the numbers each day continued to grow. But the tenacious and thankless service of these people surely demands recognition.

Not heroes of the uprising. But heroes in their own right nevertheless.

In der Heim: Field trip participant, Julie, stands on the first floor of a tenement building on Zakatno Street once inhabited by Jews in Tarnow. It was last occupied just before the liquidation of the ghetto.

In the echoes
of the
stone steps
and
darkened
corridors,
the fear of their
final hours
lingers on.

'in der Heim'

'In der Heim…' - 'in the homeland…' - words so often spoken by Yiddish speakers who left Eastern Europe at the turn of the century and still by survivors of the *shtetls* today. A strange kind of nostalgia surrounds these words. At once full of fond memories and also of bitterness. The fondness comes from the overwhelming security of *shtetl* life; the closeness, the warmth of family and the richness of tradition. And with it goes the bitter gall of prejudice, isolation and the ever impending threat of pogroms.

In a way the nostalgia is justified. *'Der Heim'* was where Yiddish culture flourished, it was where life took on a rhythm, a momentum of its own. It is where there were sufficient numbers to feel safe, even when it was not, and where you were proud to be a Jew, even when you had enemies. Life was not necessarily good in *der Heim*, but the Jews were good for life. They created richness in the midst of poverty, warmth in the coldness of winter, and they continued to pray when it might have been easier not to.

Today what is left of *der Heim* are a few dilapidated apartments only fit for pulling down. Like a bad memory, any nostalgia loses itself in the crumbling brickwork and rusting balustrades. It is a world that cannot be recreated. It evolved here, and now it is gone.

You can accept times changing and people moving on, but most of the occupants of these dwellings never chose to change or move on. In the echoes of the stone steps and darkened corridors, the fear of their final hours lingers on.

And so the tragedy of their sudden and cruel departure remains, and *der Heim* is no longer.

Dr Jonathan Webber with members of a Tempus student trip in the fields at Bobowa, from where the Bobowa Hasidic group derives its origins.

Matzevot in the Jewish cemetery above the village of Bobowa, in scenery typical of the Galician countryside.

mezuzah

Absence

I looked for you.
You were not there.
I called to you,
And through the veil
Faint echoes of absence,
In the mists of time.

Like vapour
I saw you,
Then you were gone.
And the demons of time
Laugh in my face.
Soon, even your absence
Will vanish.

S.D. Smith

Absence, it seems, is the shadow of presence.

There is nothing more telling than the chiselled-out angled rectangle in the door posts of houses where once hung a *mezuzah*. It is unashamedly a space that should be filled. That subsequent owners have failed to replace, replenish or restore the doorframes of their homes since their Jewish predecessors 'left' is surprising enough. To find that this is commonplace demonstrates just how unconcerned many of the population really are.

Like ghosts, these strange absences are there, but there is nothing to see. They tell you who once inhabited this home, but reveal nothing about them.

In the search for clues to the Jewish past, in the blanket of silence that otherwise exists, this simple absence speaks so much about what once was there.

What happened to all the *mezuzot*? Perhaps some departing Jews took their *mezuzah* with them; the majority presumably did not. Unless I am mistaken, many were simply removed and thrown away; the owners never came back for them - for certain.

The tell-tale sign of a removed *mezuzah*. Zakatno Street, Tarnow

They
are
gone
and
will
never
return.

sukkah

You build a house to live in it.

Sukkot - tabernacles - a festival of rejoicing, when temporary dwellings are constructed as in the days of sojourn in the wilderness. These are constructions to be lived in just for a while, for a moment of remembrance and thanksgiving.

If ever there was a sign of the temporary nature of Jewish domicile, it is here. A street once alive with the comings and goings of Jewish life now only sees Jews with cameras around their necks or with clipboards, taking notes. This house was once the home of a family, sufficiently concerned about the festival of sukkot to build their own *sukkah* on the roof. The construction is quite clearly seen - angle iron bolted to the side walls in order to put up the temporary structure once a year. The space between the buildings, open to the skies, once saw mothers rushing around, fathers praying and children playing under the stars. Its present owners have a balcony. Convenient.

It is difficult to describe a street once virtually totally occupied by Jews, with all the signs of their former occupancy, and yet to see no Jews in it. There is a hollowness, not because of the buildings themselves, but because as you walk here you know what happened here. It is tragedy before your eyes. No Jews live here now. In actual fact there are no Jews to live here. Like a body without a soul, this street and thousands like it have lost those for whom they were made.

Sukkah, Zakatno Street, in the old Jewish quarter of Tarnow.

hide and seek

You cannot be saved from forgetfulness.

R. Yehuda Ben Tibbon

The wheels of life keep turning.

Mothers hang out the washing and look on while their children play. Hide and seek is a language, or at least part of the language of growing up. One shows ability to hide, the other to find. And so children play hide and seek around the *bimah* of the synagogue. Of course the synagogue no longer remains, just the strong brick pillars of the *bimah*, which survived Nazi detonation. They stand tall, the symbol of a once proud community, a memorial to what once was, but is now just a place where children grow up and play games.

The irony is painful; a child growing up on 'Jewish Street', playing around the pillars of the *bimah*, oblivious of the environment she inhabits. Of course no harm is meant; but harm is done. This memorial is no sanctuary of respect, nor will it ever be. Jews only visit it from abroad; busloads of Israeli teenagers or studious researchers of the Holocaust. It has meaning only for those who care about it. And that is where it ends. Otherwise it is no more than open space among crowded houses and tenements.

So too, the fish market of Kazimierz, once buzzing with thousands of *shabbes* shoppers, now makes do with the daily humdrum of passing trade. 'Fried Fish', states the sign above the door. As a kind of Charade, things carry on with a semblance of normality. But really it is not, and cannot be the same fried fish of generations past.

Smazone Ryby (Fried Fish): Survivor, Michael Lee, enters the old Jewish fish market. Kazimierz, Krakow.

Like a game, Poles and Jews too play hide and seek; each hiding from the other. Locals pretend not to notice you, but all the time hide behind the stereotypes of Jews they hold. And Jews who come to visit hide behind the tragedy which separates them from their Polish hosts. It is not easy, and it never will be. For this little girl to understand where she is playing, her parents must first respect it. It seems that will only happen when each comes out from hiding and starts to build respect for the other.

Hide and seek: Child playing around the remnant of t
bimah in the *Alte Shul* (Old Synagogue). Tarnc

shadows of the past

A derelict Yeshivah in Kazimierz, Krakow

past and

Past and present are inseparable here.

At one corner a derelict Yeshiva lies in ruins; around another, the few surviving members of the Jewish community go to pray.

There is something enormously moving and tragically real about praying in synagogue in Poland today. Jewish prayer is Jewish prayer. It matters little where you are when you pray; except that here it is different. Here, prayers are more than the humdrum rhythm of everyday life. They are like embers of millions of prayers which could have been, maybe should have been, prayed here. There is a poignancy which can only be felt among the depleted and dying remnant of Polish-Jewish religious life - and wherever the Nazis left their evil mark.

present

Tallitot: Jewish prayer shawls used each day at the Remuh synagogue, Kazimierz, Krakow.

Not that the old Jews who remain are perfect - far from it. Trying to make ends meet, keeping up a synagogue and maintaining a few shreds of decency in your dying days are difficult enough feats to achieve. How much more so when you have been undervalued and overwhelmed by life's bitter experiences. No, the old Jews of Poland are not to be noted for their piety, or at least not for their holiness, but for their resilience. They are the faint shadows of what once was. They survived the Holocaust, resisted post-Holocaust state sponsored antisemitism, and still have the courage to pray.

And you wonder how they do it.

and
the
band
plays
on

Some try to come to terms with what has happened. Others try not to think about it.

Each night, as Yiddish music filters across the Szeroka square in Kazimierz, something from an echo of the past is relived. In the melody of the fiddler, there is now the haunting lament of destruction. There is also the terrible knowledge that anything happening here is at best the faint shadow of its former self, or worse, a mocking mimicry, or most tragic of all, the insulting imposition of kitsch commercialism.

'On the right you will see the former site of...' How many times do you hear this? It's all gone now, and everything you recreate, you impose. What right do we have to play the music of a lost generation? But then what happens if we do not, and even the faint echoes of that world are also lost? The irony is, if no one visited these places, we would feel betrayed by their apathy. When they come they create demand; which insults our sensitivities. Finding the balance is always going to be difficult. Everyone will feel something different. Some people will understand the silence and the emptiness, others need to hear the noise and have something to direct them about how to think and feel.

It is not the noise, nor the music, nor the tours that really speak here. It is the silence. How do a few hundred Jews and a few hundred tourists in Krakow replace the sixty thousand who lived their everyday lives here? How do a few thousand people in Warsaw replace the vibrancy of Yiddish culture and the varieties of Jewish life which existed there? Where are the communities of Galicia? Where are the *Yeshivahs* and the *heders*, the theatres and the taverns, the schools and the sports clubs? Where are the imposing *shuls* and the little *stibls*? Where are the Zionists and the Bundists, the *Hasidim* and the secularists, the wealthy and the *schnorers*?

Gone. They are all gone.

Fiddler: Tomasz Kukurba, violinist and vocalist of the *Klezmer* band 'Kroke'. Kukurba, like many young Poles, discovered his Jewish roots as a young adult. Now with colleagues Tomasz Lato and Jerzy Bawol, they create and perform a new and powerful sound in *Klezmer*, reflecting the struggle and sorrow of the post-Holocaust Jewish experience in Poland.

Onlooker: local woman looks on as a small group of Jewish tourists photograph a synagogue.

Office block: The main synagogue in Sieradz now houses a number of local businesses.

Gallows: A Star of David on a gallows, painted on the side of the Izaaka Synagogue, Kazimierz. Subsequently whitewashed, its shadow is still clearly visible.

whitewash

'Maybe now Poland will at last understand that villainy and holiness dwell in one house...'

Andrzej Szczypiorski

You can try to paint it over, but antisemitism is not about to go away.

The roots of European antisemitism, deeply embedded in the origins of Christianity, have been woven into the fabric of our so-called civilised world. What began as a crusade to invalidate the older tradition ended in the bloodshed of a thousand years of violence against the Jews, wherever they have been in Christendom.

Today the saga is far from over. Now, more complex than ever before, antisemitism has influenced developments in the modern world and has been influenced by it. It even inhabits the crevices of our postmodern environment, where once again a basic ignorance and misunderstanding of the Jewish experience persists at worrying levels.

Nowhere more so than in Poland where, since the Holocaust, Jews have been driven out of their jobs and homes. Poles most certainly do not drink in antisemitism with their mothers' milk, any more than Jews are born bankers, but there is a deeply ingrained enmity which makes even the most optimistic worry about the future.

Here in Poland, religious, political and racial motivations stimulate antisemitism. It is used to gain power, to take power, to accuse your enemy, and to insult your friend. It is preached and taught, hurled and whispered. When you wish to assert your Polishness, you vocalise your dislike of the Jews. Poland would not be Poland as we know it without antisemitism.

This cannot be whitewashed. You cannot paint it over and hope it will all go away. It must be faced, and those brave enough to start should be given all the help that can be found. In Poland today there are people with insights into the Jewish experience who are there to help. They understand the problem, but need supporting too. These few courageous souls need friends to help them if they are to change the opinion of a nation. Because antisemitism is a problem does not mean everyone is an antisemite. Those who are not hold the key to the future.

If the Holocaust is a warning from history, then heeding that warning, and finding the right partners to work with, is surely the beginning to the end of an age-old problem.

Sporting antisemitism: Widzew, the football team you do not support - they must be Jews.

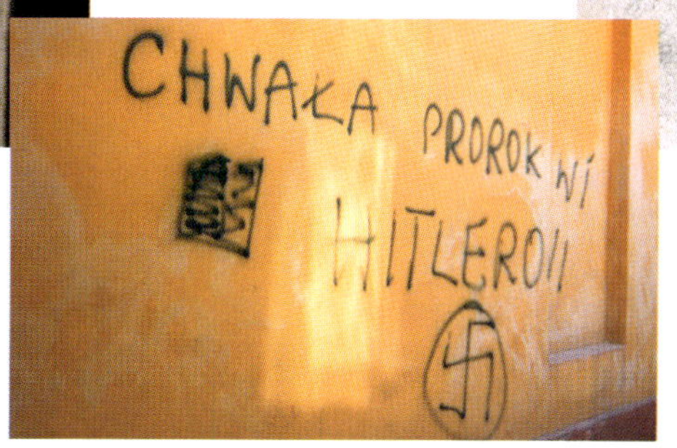

'Glory to the prophets of Hitler.'

'Gypsies to the Gas': Gypsies, still a minority in Poland, receive substantial racial hatred, as is the case in many European countries today.

'Polska': Star of David mural in derelict synagogue on Dabrowa Tarnowska, with 'Poland' scrawled boldly across it.

where memories

meet

second death

'Memory is the keyword.
To remember is to create links between past and present,
between past and future.
To remember is to affirm man's faith in humanity
- in spite of itself -
and to confer meaning to our fleeting endeavours.'

Elie Wiesel

This is the Holocaust.

The shocking thing is just how beautiful this place is. Some eight thousand Jewish people were murdered here. Eight hundred of them were children. The trees have grown here for decades. Now I stand under them, bemused by many sensations; beauty and peacefulness, terror and overwhelming emotion. It is impossible to imagine. Under these trees people were made to line up or lie down and be shot. Under these trees, children who never had the chance to make anything of their lives were simply shot because they were born to the 'wrong' parents in the 'wrong' year and happened to be in the 'wrong' place when the Germans made their mark.

This is the Holocaust; men, women, and children murdered in obscurity. There are no graves, except mass graves. There are no names, no faces and no memory. Try as you might, you cannot remember someone you never knew. This is dying the second death: absolute obscurity.

Children: The entrance to a mass grave, dedicated to the memory of the eight hundred children murdered here.

As with many such sites, it is more complex than it first appears. There were also Polish 'politicals' murdered here. The tragedy of their deaths is equally great, because each murder is as evil as the next. Some of these individuals have names, though. The names of those from Nowy Sacz are inscribed on a plaque below a crucifix. They have memory - because even I know who they are, although I never knew them.

For the Jews who are no longer here to mourn their dead, these are the forgotten places, wherein even memory cannot dwell. There is silence and only silence. The struggle against the success of the 'Final Solution' is the struggle against obfuscation. It is the struggle to name, individualise and in some way bring back the memory of the forgotten.

In the face of eternal loss, that remains a duty.

this
is
the
holocaust

Mass death: Standing under the trees at Zbylitowska Gora, where eight thousand Jews and two thousand Poles were murdered.

the parting of the ways

This is where it all ended.

This is where mothers parted from children, fathers from brothers and husbands from wives. This is where some lived and most were murdered. This is where humanity and morality parted, where success was the antonym of human decency, and depravity was the norm. This is Birkenau.

Birkenau, a place wherein history, memory, symbol and commerce collide. It is both banal and intensely evil. It is absolutely imperative to understand, but very few do. Birkenau is not just about railway lines, fences, gate towers and piles of shoes. Birkenau is a complex set of historical circumstances; it has inherent values and anti-values, and most of all it is at the tragic fulcrum of many people's experiences.

One thing must remain in our thoughts always; Birkenau is a place where over a million individuals were murdered. Its soil is soaked in the blood and tears of human suffering and remains their final resting-place. They did not choose it, but their lives were ended here.

Birkenau should not become a cliché of human bestiality and depravity. It should always be remembered and understood as a place where such cruelties actually took place. If we can now cope with mass death and talk freely about the minutiæ of murder without losing sleep, then we need to be warned. Birkenau, Belzec, Chelmno, Majdanek, Sobibor and Treblinka are not places to grow used to.

Points: Evil is not banal, but the banal reality of this evil is summed up in the points on the ramp. Innocuous enough, but someone planned the layout down to its last detail. Who decided, one wonders, what points to use, where to use them and to what effect?

The final road: The railway line and the gate tower of Auschwitz-Birkenau have become symbols of the Holocaust. For me, this little path has even more meaning. Before the 'ramp' was even built, over half the Jewish victims of Auschwitz, some seven hundred and fifty thousand people, trudged along this muddy footpath to the camp. This was the final road for many. It is not the structures nor the rails that count, but the people who passed this way, one by one.

Try to look,
just try and see.

Charlotte Delbo

Parting of the ways: A piece of track on the 'ramp' at Auschwitz-Birkenau. Visitors have placed stones at the junction as it is the tradition to place stones on Jewish headstones. What struck me here was the human experience of parting. Hundreds of thousands of husbands and wives, brothers and sisters, parents and children parted here for ever. The track is my visual reference. It is not the track that I am photographing, but that and those which it speaks of.

they came alone *together*

Nothing hides the truth of the Holocaust more than numbers.

'Six million' as a number means very little to me. Then try to imagine human lives. One million, two hundred thousand victims of Birkenau also means very little, particularly if you try to imagine one individual, and still fail to comprehend the experience. The real tragedy of Birkenau is that each person was an individual, with a name, a family, a home, gifts and talents, virtues and vices. They were not an indecipherable homogeneous group of despised Jews, herded to their deaths, numbered, calculated and accounted for. That is how the Nazis saw them.

In our imaginations we have to juggle both the scale and anonymity of the Holocaust, with the millions of individual tragedies this represents. Mass murder should not become an excuse to avoid the detail, but an incentive to discover it. Our memorialisation should not bow to the system the Nazis created, but personalise the impersonal, give dignity where there was shame, create honour where there was disgrace and give a sense of humanity in the face of the baseless process of dehumanisation imposed upon these individuals.

Birkenau is not just an historical site of interest, a kind of case study for students of the period. It is not just 'a warning from history', nor 'a lesson for today', nor is it a 'symbol of our times'. Birkenau and the death camps of the 'Final Solution' are not contained nor explained by our clichés. They should challenge the very fundamental nature of human experience, and provoke the most personal questions. They should leave you asking 'Who am I?' and 'What am I capable of?' And they should leave you unable to answer anything.

We watched stunned... Two people, two worlds, who have occupied a place in the human scheme, who have lived, existed, acted and created. Who have laboured for the world and for themselves, laid a brick on the great edifice, woven a thread for the world for the future - and in only twenty minutes no vestige of them remains.

Salmen Gradowski.
Member of the Sonderkommando
in the crematoria
at Birkenau.

They came alone: Nathan wanders along the length of the 'ramp' at Birkenau, deep in thought.

things to remember

Memory and the skin of memory. It clings to me yet.

Charlotte Delbo

This is all that remains.

Knives, forks, spoons, shoes, shaving brushes, tooth brushes, hair brushes, hair. It is raining and the rusting pile of metallic objects rots slowly in the open air. They have been left where they lay. Like corpses, they are lifeless. They are no longer spoons used as spoons, but spoons like a pile of *matzevot*, memorials to their anonymous owners. No one knows who owned them, but we can be all but certain they were Jews who packed them in their cases with the uneasy confidence that they would soon be using them at their destination.

Not so. They were piled high, a mountain of them, then they were sorted. Today, just a few remain. They are survivors of a sort; they tell a terrible tale and bear witness for their long departed owners. They are bridges between our imagination and the reality. They are the decaying link between the impossible and its comprehension.

Things to remember…

My dolly,
A diary,
That frayed red ribbon,
The pencil chewed at the end.
A needle and thread
And a thimble too.
My shells from the sea last year,
A small glass bead,
For mummy to wear.
A photo of granny,
My puppy dog's hair,
A knife,
A fork,
A spoon.

S.D. Smith

On the receiving end: Kitty Hart-Moxon describes life in the *Kanada* section sorting the belongings of recently arrived inmates.

Things to remember: Cutlery in the open air at the *Kanada* section of Auschwitz-Birkenau.

Barracks: Arek Hersh describes life in the barracks. Inmates packed in, six to a bunk, groan as they die in the chill of the night. We stand and listen to his words, and try to imagine.

Really, one cannot.

Admin: The hut on the 'ramp' where SS officers went about their daily routine.

Block 25: In the Women's Camp, women selected to die waited here for certain death.

beyond imagination

'How did I keep alive in Auschwitz? My principle is: myself first, second, and third. Then nothing. Then myself again - then all the others.'

Ena Weiss

You lived here for some time, and then you died here; that was the order of things.

One set of people made nothing by another. The victors, the strong, relegated the vanquished to no more than vermin. They tore them out of their beds, packed them like sardines and shipped them to who knows where. Then they killed them and enslaved the few they chose to spare.

Today, it is all so neat and tidy here; ordinary almost. Nobody is dying, nobody fearing the moment which follows. In the haze of emotions, you only want to be alone, at a place where a thousand people were crammed into a building made for fifty-two horses. Everything is silent, even while the chattering tour groups come and go. You listen, but only hear the sound of your own footsteps. You look, but only see the empty spaces.

Birkenau, and every place like it, is beyond the imagination of all, save for those who went through it. So why come, why look and listen? Surely, you could read about it just the same. It is true, you will not know much more once you have been here. Neither will you understand it. But perhaps it is understanding how little you understand, and knowing how little you know, and struggling to find words... when words lose their meaning. That lets you know what is significant here, where you are. Only if you leave knowing and understanding have you wasted your time.

The contrasts are telling here. There is Block 25, where women were crowded in with no food, no water, no sanitation and no air, waiting for inevitable death. Then there is the cool normality of the administration hut on the 'ramp', where the masters of death brewed their coffee, smoked their lights and filled out their paperwork from the latest transport. Were they convinced of what they were doing? So it appears. They were certainly comfortable with it.

Murder became routine. Do we know what this means?

the here and now

Birkenau is not what it was.

Today, flowers grow and birds sing. Then, they did not. Flowers growing out of blood-soaked soil. The memory of death, covered by a carpet of delicate blooms. Birkenau is a meadow of varied flora, buzzing with the activity of its accompanying fauna. Beetles, grasshoppers, ladybirds and the constant melody of skylarks.

One hundred and twenty thousand inmates were crammed onto this site. In summer, hot, dusty and barren. In the dead of winter it was hard as rock. The rest of the year it was mud.

Still you sense its unforgiving nature. The flat boggy site makes the most of the weather; chilling in winter, even mild misty days seem to soak one to the bone. Intensely hot in summer, there is no shade as the sun climbs high in the sky. Today we visit in our warm winter coats or wear our shades and sun block. Then, even the sun was your enemy as thirst and dehydration combined in the heat of the day. Then, the cutting winds of winter left thousands for dead; and their memory is no more.

There is nothing more fitting than the peacefulness, the quiet, the winter snow, the summer meadow. And yet it prevents you ever understanding.

'I see mud, just a sea of mud.'

Kitty Hart-Moxon

Mud, a sea of mud: Flowers growing at Auschwitz-Birkenau today.

auschwitz

memory is

They are the drowned... we are the saved.

Primo Levi

Memory is, whereas memorials give form to experience.

You can create an image, but whether it will ever be understood is another matter altogether. You can put up a monument, but the danger is that with the passage of time its significance might change. We have created monumental societies, in which at every site of historical significance we place an image or an obelisk, a plaque or a memorial. Then we ask what they mean; and too few can tell us.

History is not about chronicling dates, times, facts and places. History is about how we interpret those events. To this end, the Holocaust is not over. Not only does its memory linger deep in the hearts of those who survived, but as we struggle to interpret events, its history is still being made.

Memory and memorial: Survivor Michael Lee wanders across the front of the memorial at Auschwitz-Birkenau at the end of the ramp where his family were selected to die.

'Mainly Jews': The memorial inscriptions at Auschwitz-Birkenau indicate that it was 'mainly Jews' who were murdered there. The monument itself bears two insignia, a triangle, indicating the political prisoners of Auschwitz, and a Polish cross.

There is no substitute for experience. The image of a lone survivor wandering in front of the memorial at Auschwitz-Birkenau demonstrates the contrast between experience and interpretation. The monument attempts to demonstrate that something significant happened here. It is a symbol of historical experience. The monument bears witness to the significance of events, it provokes, it cajoles and it represents the perspective of its creators. The presence of the survivor brings to that monument a dimension it can never have and never will. The survivor is the one who, as the exception, bears witness to that which the Nazis intended should never have been told.

He just is, and in so being, bears witness for those who cannot.

a million matzevot

Why should I bless his name?
The Eternal,
Lord of the Universe,
the All-Powerful and Terrible,
was silent.
What had I to thank Him for?

Elie Wiesel

A million *matzevot:* At points around Auschwitz-Birkenau where human ashes were deposited, black granite headstones are placed.
They read: 'To the memory of the men, women and children who fell victims to the Nazi genocide. Here lie their ashes. May their souls rest in peace.'

Cemeteries without gravestones. That is what Belzec, Birkenau, Chelmno, Majdanek, Sobibor and Treblinka really are.

If you were to place a headstone for each individual who was murdered here, the endless sea of stones would sharply bring into focus what these places mean as sites of mass death.

So often people think of Poland as being a large Jewish cemetery. In a way it is. But we should ask ourselves whether such places as this are worthy of such an honourable title. At a cemetery you visit the individual grave of an individual person. There is a name, a date of birth and a date of death. In a cemetery, you remember the individual with respect, with a sense of the past and that individual's contribution to it.

At Birkenau there are only ashes. Stop to think about the rites of death and mourning in the Jewish tradition, and you quickly realise what a desecration this place really is. Murder, for a start. The indignity of mass death, unclothed and ashamed while praying the *Sh'ma Israel* or clinging hopelessly to your loved ones. Then the debasement of 'ritual cleansing' Nazi style. Cremation; forbidden by Jewish law and avoided by most Jews still today. An individual burial; with family and friends to sit *shivah* for a week, then to mourn their loss for a year? Most of these Jews were gone with no one to mourn them by dawn the next day. And then the issues of human remains; so important to gather them up and place them safely in the earth where they belong. They were thrown to the wind, and into the rivers, used for fertiliser, left piled on the earth exposed to the wind and the rain.

A cemetery; we would that it was. Still, it is the final resting place of these forgotten souls and should always be treated as such.

The best of intentions: Young people working to clear the field of ashes at the back of Birkenau wished to commemorate the victims by placing Stars of David and crosses on the site. The result - confused symbolism at best. Now removed, the issue demonstrated how difficult it is to find a meaningful means of expression at 'Auschwitz'.

Crematorium II: Birkenau: Blown up by the Nazis before their retreat from south-west Poland.
The white roses on the concrete caught my eye. It is not typical for Jews to leave flowers, so these may not have been left by Jewish visitors, but they were obviously bought specially and laid with meaning and care

the places
wherein the Jewish soul
of Europe
was murdered

in the rubble of my mind

The fire burns boldly, calmly. Nothing stands in its way, nothing puts it out.

Salmen Gradowski

Twisted metal, broken concrete and roses: the contrasts of Birkenau.

Rarely does one think of a pile of rubble being a place of honour for the dead. The remains of the gas chambers and crematoria, now no more than broken masonry, are the only objects left to remind one what actually happened here. They are historical site, demolition site and memorial in one.

When the Germans retreated from the eastern territories, by and large they were successful in removing the evidence of their crimes. At Birkenau, the permanence of the fixtures they created only allowed them to destroy the building, but not to remove its traces. They had been too confident, too assured of success and too convinced of the efficacy of their endeavours to make something temporary.

Designed, improved and redesigned, the five gas chambers and crematoria of the two main Auschwitz complex sites were made to last. It is difficult to know what the intentions were once the Jews were done with, but certainly these industrial units were created with the future in mind. Neither the best workmanship nor the best materials were used, but they were efficient and did the job they were designed to do.

Outside these derelict structures, hundreds of thousands of people had queued patiently, unaware of the imminent fate that awaited them. Bemused by the contradictions of a friendly welcome, comforting words, the increasingly ominous signs and smells of death, they filed into the buildings and never re-emerged.

The ruins of the crematoria are more than destroyed architectural artefacts. They are memorials in their own right, the place - no more than a pile of rubble - wherein the Jewish soul of Europe was murdered.

Crematorium IV, Birkenau: This crematorium was destroyed during a prisoner revolt on 7 October 1944. While the killing had all but ceased by that time, still the triumph of revolt was significant, then and now.

in my backyard

Number 17: Timetable for the Oswiecim bus route.

Birkenau is on the Number 17 bus route.

It is also in the backyard of the villagers of Brzezinka - renamed Birkenau by the Germans. People work here, shop here, learn here and pray here. They ride their bikes, mow their lawns and milk their cows. They also catch the bus to Oswiecim by the barracks of BIIa, that's the way it is here.

In one way the acceptance of this monstrous carbuncle in their back yard is understandable, if unacceptable. Who would like to contemplate the meaning of Birkenau every day of their life? Simple folk certainly do not wish to have their lives disturbed by the historic significance of a factory of death in their quiet little village. But sadly the attitude is coloured by other opinions.

More troubling is the apparent lack of mutual understanding between those who live there and those who come to visit. Belligerence is not always the word, but disregard, or cynicism, often is. Bus loads of camera-wielding tourists arriving every day are bound to have some impact on the local attitude, but there is also the feeling that they think they know better. This in turn leads to the tragic stand-off which takes place so often here.

Birkenau is not a short cut to the shops, nor a place to run the dog, nor to teach your children how to ride their bikes. But, sadly, each of these happens.

All in a day's work: A grinning local worker takes his tractor to mow grass at Birkenau.

Shopping trip: Local residents cross the site of Birkenau on their return journey from the shops.

There is little doubt about it, the Auschwitz complex is a major tourist attraction. Is this a problem, or is it how we handle it which makes it so?

If Oswieçim was one of the least desirable destinations on the European continent earlier this century, today it attracts a considerable crowd of visitors eager to see what happened there. Concern over the trappings of commercialisation is not misplaced. Over half a million visitors a year provide a ready market for additional merchandise and service. But in criticising it one must also remember it is a valuable opportunity to bring to the attention of the visiting public the meaning of this place in history and in human conscience.

What is an appropriate way to meet the physical needs of individuals - who have not come there to suffer - without turning the place into a destination with all amenities provided to make the day an enjoyable experience?

The answer lies in the atmosphere you create. If you provide hot dogs and ice creams, then people will assume you wish them to be bought and consumed there. If you provide a *bureau de change* and a post office, then visitors will change money and send postcards. There is no doubt, however, that these services demean the seriousness of the occasion. Visiting the Auschwitz museum should not simply be a day out. The human consequences of its historical meaning, and the implications for contemporary society, are such that only to add it to your list of interesting holidays for after-dinner conversation is an insult to the dead.

Visiting Auschwitz should jolt every individual's sense of reality - whoever they are and whatever their perspective. All who come should be prepared to be confronted. The problem is, of course, Auschwitz means different things to different people.

For Jews coming here it can be a place of personal pilgrimage, to see where members of their family were murdered. It can also be to grapple with their Jewish identity or to make a statement about Jewish continuity in spite of it. Jews come to mourn, to learn and to think about their own lives in the shadow of such tragedy.

For Poles, Auschwitz is also a site of martyrdom. During the first year of the establishment of the camp in 1940, most of the twenty thousand internees were Poles. During that year it gained its infamy among the Polish people, which continued even after the mass murder of the Jews. Still today the largest number of visitors to the site are Polish school children, learning Polish history. Should they not come? Of course they should; but there should be a shared memory rather than a divided memory of Auschwitz.

Then the tourists come too. Among them Germans, Russians, Dutch, French, English and American sightseers eager to get a glimpse of this black spot of world history. And so they come, take their photos, shake their heads and clamber back onto their coaches. And the 650,000 Jews of Belzec, the 220,000 Jews of Chelmno, the 300,000 Jews of Majdanek, the 300,000 Jews of Sobibor, the 850,000 Jews of Treblinka and the countless thousands shot in the forests of Europe are largely forgotten.

Auschwitz has only become the symbol it is because of the mass murder of European Jewry. Polish school children would still visit Auschwitz as a concentration camp, and it would remain important to a sense of their own history, even had the Jews not been murdered there in such numbers. But as a site symbolising the destruction of European Jewry, it must always be seen alongside and as a part of all the other forgotten places where most of the six million died, unknown and unknowable.

smile please! you are at auschwitz

'Of too much was our talk of too little.'

Paul Celan

Peace process: A Polish Catholic from the village of Brzezinka, comes 'to pray for peace' - and simultaneously to condemn 'the Jews' for trying to usurp the memory of Polish martyrs on this site.

mixed

Generations come

and generations go,

but contention lasts forever.

Ahad Ha'am

metaphors

When Pope John Paul II went to the site of Auschwitz I in 1979, he celebrated mass by a large cross. (It is now situated on an adjacent site, not far from Block 11, the Block of Death.) He prayed for the souls of the dead and he prayed for peace and reconciliation. He also made reference to Auschwitz being the 'martyrdom of Christ being recapitulated in the mass murder of the Jews'.

The symbolism is strong. It is also Christian, and highly problematic. However well it was intended, unwittingly the Pope opened up a Pandora's Box of controversy. Shortly afterward, taking his message of prayer and contemplation seriously, a group of Carmelite nuns moved into a disused building near the site.

There is no reason why Christian believers should not pray for peace and for the souls of those who perished; but there are a few complications. The site they chose to occupy was once a building used by the SS for storing Zyklon B. The presence of a twenty-foot cross infuriated some members of the Jewish community, who felt it was an unnecessary and insensitive imposition. Now the slogan 'Defend the Cross' has resulted in the erection of many crosses on that piece of ground, in order to defy the Jewish wish for the cross to be removed. In the fallout from the ensuing conflict, the nuns built and moved to a brand new convent a short distance away. But the cross remains, and continues to irk those for whom such symbolism is an affront.

The rights and wrongs of the argument are not the material of this study. Both sides want the sensitivities of their memory and their particular way of expressing it respected. However, there is something of an imbalance in sensitivity at the moment.

It is strange that though ninety-five percent of the victims were Jewish, the only religious symbol you will find at Auschwitz is a cross.

'Remembering. We are': A placard of Pope John Paul II fixed to the fence confronts the visitor with the challenge of Polish national memory.

Candles: This candle was lit in the barracks of Birkenau. While there were many Christians incarcerated in the camp, the majority in Birkenau were Jewish. Naturally, to Jewish visitors such symbolism is an affront to their whole purpose of being at Birkenau. For Christians, it is the only way they know.

Convent: The building used by the Carmelites, empty now but still causing controversy.

peripheral matters

Its not always what you see, but what you do not, which matters.

Around the periphery of Auschwitz I are a number of places which have profound impact on the meaning of the complex as a whole. Most visitors to the site do not know they are there, and hence do not visit them.

Auschwitz was a sprawling complex, a network of camps, factories and territories, with many buildings outside the fences themselves. In total, it covered some forty-four square kilometres. Just two hundred yards away from the museum is a mass grave dug by the Soviets to bury dead inmates found in January 1945 when the camp was discovered.

This is one of the few sites around the complex where you can see the final resting-place of *any* of the inmates of the camp. Jews and Christians were buried side by side in separate coffins, and they were given a Christian burial. Today, a single cross stands in a walled off garden beside the road and the bus repair garage.

A little further along the road there is the villa of Rudolf Hoess, its long garden stretching back to the territory of Auschwitz I. The present occupants have a clear view of Crematorium I from their bean patch.

As well as the former Carmelite Convent, there are several less well-known churches around the area of the camps. Each day at five o'clock, once the tourists have gone home, the church behind the car park rings its bells to call the faithful to prayer. At Birkenau, the former SS headquarters is now a Catholic church which declares its hope for peace under a banner stating that 'Jesus is the only way!'

Plans for a supermarket in the environs may have appeared unseemly and were scrapped. It is questionable how much more seemly it is to have a hot dog stall, an ice cream kiosk, a bus depot and half a dozen churches in the area.

Bean patch: View of Crematorium I from Rudolf Hoess' villa. The present occupants still have a clear view through their bean patch.

A good Christian burial: Inmates buried together by local Catholic priests after the liberation.

'Ave Maria': Each day the faithful are called to mass behind the car park at Auschwitz I.

'Jesus is the only way!': This church, just outside Auschwitz-Birkenau, is situated in the old SS headquarters and proclaims its message of evangelism to all who pass by.

Lake of ashes: Here, among other places, the ashes of victims were deposited at Auschwitz-Birkenau.

in the silence

Above the clamour of the tourism and
the din of competing voices,
the silence and the stillness have more
meaning than any words.

shoes and ashes

'Answers: I say there are none.'

Elie Wiesel

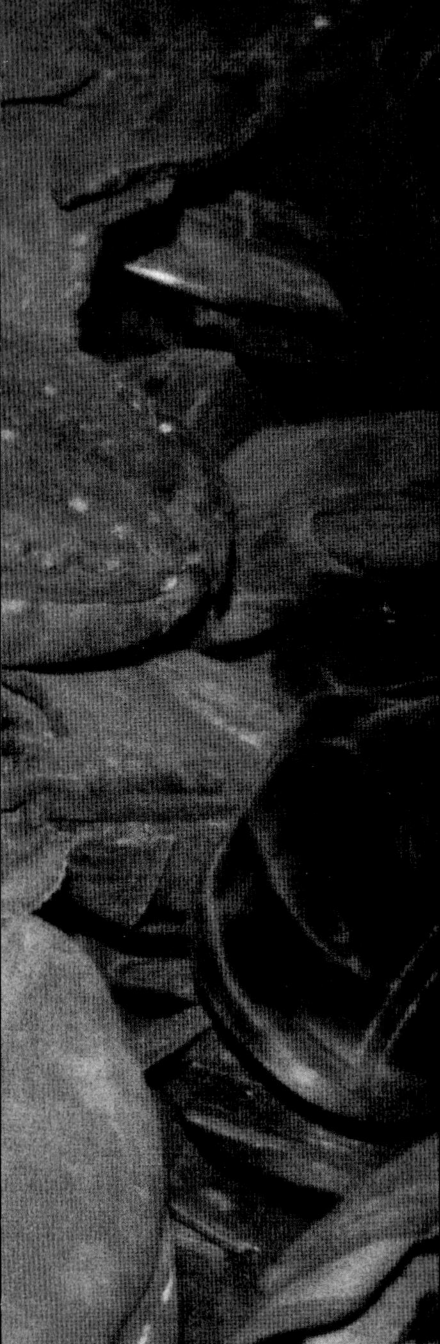

Majdanek is not about symbols, tourism, churches, mass murder, memory or peace.

This is a site of enormous historical significance, not visited by hundreds and thousands of people, lacking in basic facilities and unsophisticated in every way. Away from the din of the multitudes and the clamour of controversy, Majdanek is also a place with many memories, but here, as yet, they do not compete. Jews were Jews, Poles, Poles, and Soviets, Soviets. They lived here, they died here, they were all victims of National Socialism here. In a way it is easier to understand because the numbers are lower and the spaces less far-flung. Majdanek usually has more impact on visitors than Auschwitz, simply because its lack of symbolism creates no prior illusions or expectations. Majdanek delivers all the impact of Auschwitz - but as yet without the symbolism.

In a way, Majdanek is all the more horrifying for that.

If anything must be said, and an image has to be conveyed, it is the shoes that mean most to me here. Shoes. Thousands upon thousands of them, caged up, smelling of the slow decay of rotting leather. Big shoes and little shoes, men's shoes, women's shoes and children's shoes.

They came here expecting to live here.

And they died here.

suffer *little children*

It was the end of a long day. The sun was setting in the evening sky, its warmth making the red brick bell tower glow orange. It was a beautiful little church, its neatly trimmed lawns and pansy beds kept meticulously by the nuns from the adjoining convent. The old chestnut tree had seen the faithful pass by to pray, day in, day out, for decades. Christ hung from his cross above the doorway, looking down as we peered through the locked gates. Christ and the chestnut tree had seen other things too.

One day in August 1942, one thousand four hundred Jews were crammed into the church and held overnight. Men, women and children, they had neither food nor water as they awaited their fate. The next day they were all taken to Chelmno and murdered.

It was not the nuns who did this, of course; it was the Germans. There is little doubt that this is the most significant thing ever to have happened in this church. Yet today there is not so much as a mention of it in the church itself.

Strangely though, there is a plaque commemorating a schoolmaster, Feliks Binkowski, a Polish Catholic, who died in Dachau several weeks later. Surely Christ's faithful could find it in their hearts to commemorate the loss of over one thousand innocent lives? Surely are not the Jews of Sieradz worth even a mention?

Prayers at the altar: A lengthy discussion on the altar about candles, between nuns and their assistants at the church in Sieradz.

Christ and the chestnut tree had seen other things too.

Chance: Arek Hersh was just a child when he left his mother and siblings inside the church to go to beg the soldiers for water. He never went back in, as he was ordered to join some men selected to work. He survived. His family were murdered at Chelmno the following day.

Ignorance is (not) bliss.

Popular, adapted

each to his own

Some seek solace by reciting Kaddish and lighting candles.

Others by finding refuge in their beloved cross.

Others pick flowers.

Memorial wall at Chelmno: More than 320,000 Jews were murdered here and buried in mass graves. The clearing in the forest is beautiful, and altogether ugly.

Kaddish: Our small group gather around the Star of David at the head of the mass grave, light a candle and recite *Kaddish*.

There is no single way to commemorate tragic events. If you are Jewish, visiting a site of mass murder where people were killed *because* they were Jewish is a difficult burden to bear. You can think, you can cry or you can pray, but to do so you have to come as close as possible to the identity of the individuals themselves. And that is not easy if you were not there. But to be there with someone who survived, who was destined to be buried in obscurity, creates a bridge between the experience and our imagination of it. To be there with someone for whom this is real, and whose family has never been mourned as they might have been, to say *kaddish* and to light candles together, becomes an unforgettably meaningful moment.

For the few Christians for whom such places are also sites of mourning and remembrance, to pray at a cross is the only way they know, and therefore the most appropriate way. When over ninety per cent of the victims were Jewish, to be confronted by a Catholic altar at Chelmno is a little unnerving. But then Catholics pray there too.

Then there are those who do not pray at all. Visiting Chelmno to pick flowers on the mass graves of murdered Jews, may appear an unseemly way to behave.

It is.

Per Deum est memoria: A Polish family comes and pays respects at the cross. Maybe their families suffered here too.

Afternoon stroll: Local women pick flowers on the mass graves of Poland's Jews.

One by one: The group arrived together, but instinctively approached the monument one at a time. This is a place to be alone with your thoughts. Here, the concept of humanity ceased to exist.

'Never were so many human lives extinguished in so short a time, and with so lucid a combination of technological ingenuity, fanaticism and cruelty.'

Primo Levi

Stones of remembrance: A field of stones recalls all the little communities, rounded up and brought here. This is where the ashes of those communities now lie.

Imagination: You will never imagine what actually happened here.

Treblinka, where over eight hundred thousand Jews were murdered in less than a year.

There is no avoiding the magnitude of this place. Along with Belzec, Chelmno and Sobibor, Treblinka epitomises the intention of the 'Final Solution'. Jews were brought here mainly from Warsaw and the Bialystok region and, with the exception of a very small number, all perished on arrival. There were no regular work *Kommandos*, no factories and virtually no chance of survival.

It was chosen as a site of mass murder because there was already a concentration camp here. This was a secluded location to which Jews could be deported so that their disappearance might go unnoticed. The local population was unconcerned about such matters and the small numbers of personnel involved meant that thousands of Jews could be murdered each day, without it ever becoming an issue.

In this way, over two million Jews were murdered at the four death camps and today, save for the sites of their destruction, there is little to show for their presence. When in Hebrew we use the term *Sho'ah*, it is this place, even more than 'Auschwitz', which comes to mind. The evidence of intent in murdering Jews as Jews was absolute. Here everything focused on murder and only murder. Here, the 'Final Solution' was final.

Now the camp, which was destroyed by the German occupiers, is difficult to imagine. The memorial is powerful. But in the beauty of the Polish forest and stillness of this God-forsaken space, no imagination can bridge the gap between life and total death that happened at Treblinka every day. It doesn't make sense. It cannot make sense.

Warsaw: A single stone today denotes that over three hundred thousand Jews were brought from the Warsaw ghetto alone.

sho'a

treblinka

Roadside vigil: The imposing monument in memory of 'the victims of Hitlerite terror', to remind all who pass by of the need to fight fascism.

Crown: The barbed wire crown fits fairly into the Christian concept of suffering.

This small monument to the Jews murdered at Plasow is tucked away out of sight of the road... and hence perceived as less important.

Unless you know the truth of this place.

At times, the monument is defaced with antisemitic graffiti.

picnic site

Not all sites of the Holocaust in Poland are death camps. There are many hundreds of concentration camps, labour camps and sites of mass execution. At Płasow, near Krakow, the infamous commandant Amon Goeth imposed his sadistic nature and cold-blooded murders.

Płasow inmates were made to work in the adjoining quarry, sent to other work camps or deported to Auschwitz or Belzec. Today, it is maintained as a site of memorial. 'Maintained' does not refer to its condition. It is untidy scrub land, undulating in places, with sharp contrasts in topography in others.

By the road there is a striking concrete memorial of five men looking down, burdened by the weight of their suffering. In Polish, to the rear, the inscription remembers the 'victims of the Hitlerite terror'.

Behind and beyond, a small stone erected in memory of the Jews persecuted there, bears witness not only to the Jews who died here but also to the inferior status of the memory of the Jews at many of these places. An afterthought; even though it *was* there first.

Catholics can pray at a large wooden cross. And those who wish to, can picnic in the open spaces.

We stopped some children who were firing at each other with toy guns and asked them if they knew what happened here. They nodded, shrugged and carried on firing anyway.

Picnic site: Local inhabitants sit on the grass and enjoy the afternoon sun.

survivor

'But he's only human and he wants to live. So he must forget.
He thanks God for what remains, and that he can forget.
And let's not talk about that.'

Michael Podchlebnik

What is there to say when you stand with a man beside a mass grave that contains his parents and siblings?

Holocaust survivor Arek Hersh stands by one of the mass graves containing the family he left behind in the Church at Sieradz, aged twelve.

Ben Helfgott: Hortensja Glass Factory, where he worked as a slave labourer. Piotrokow. The factory has since closed.

Nathan and Jill Pivnick: Bendzin, site of the former great synagogue

a

Michael Lee: Tap in the hallway just as it used to be. Lodz.

Doorway to freedom: Gina Schwarzman came to this doorway as a child being smuggled from the Radom ghetto.

Nathan Pivnick: Back in class fifty-five years on. There are no Jews in the Jewish school of Bendzin today.

Marion Turski: Today historical editor of 'Polityka', then a survivor of the Lodz ghetto and Auschwitz,

world apart

And the memory lives on. Theirs is a story that no one should ever have to tell. Buried deep in the recesses of their broken hearts are memories, which are broken too. A world apart, shattered dreams are the shards of their former lives and now there is no way back.

'Survivors', we call them. People of a different kind, and yet just like us. We know nothing of what they survived nor how. We understand so little of the pain they endured. And still do. Then, somehow, these brave souls find the courage to return to the places that left them for dead. They come to show us and to help us understand, to support us as we weep with them.

'This was my school... This was my home... This was my grandfather's factory, my uncle's shop... This is where I went through the wall... This is where I last saw my mother... This is where my father died.' One by one I hear their names; a roll call of sorrow and shame. Like a moment that's gone, the past can never be relived. But they remember, and in so doing inscribe a fragment of that past into our present.

Now the time is almost gone, and memory becomes history. But what they shared will always be remembered.

Photos: Some of the survivors who have assisted Beth Shalom trips to Poland, during which time this book was compiled.

When Past Meets Future

When past meets future
And the seas of time change,
The shadows of the nether world
Leave warm hearts
Cold as ashes.
Then old men weep
And children cease their laughter.
But out of sorrow
Hope is born,
When past meets future,
Here,
Now.

S.D. Smith

Glossary

Bimah	Podium in the synagogue where three times a week the scrolls of the Torah are taken and read to the congregation.
Hasid	(Lit.: 'Pious one') Latterly a member of the Hasidic Jewish Movement.
Hasidism	A movement started in the 17th Century by the Baal Shem Tov as a breakaway from the then Jewish orthodoxy. Today, the Hasidic movement is identified by its adherence to orthodox practices.
Hevrah Kaddishe	Jewish Burial Society. When an individual in the community dies, the *Hevrah Kaddishe* collect and prepare the body for burial and are responsible for ensuring that Jewish law is carried out from death to interment.
Kaddish	The Jewish prayer for the dead.
Kvetl'ch	(Lit.: 'Wishes') Handwritten prayers left on the graves of respected individuals, and in particular learned rabbis and teachers.
Matzevah	Jewish headstone. (Plural: *matzevot*)
Mezuzah	Small receptacle containing the biblical blessing of the *Shema Israel* and other blessings. Jewish homes have them fitted to the right-hand door post, angled inward. They are also placed on the internal doors of living rooms.
Mitzvah	A law of the Jewish faith. It also refers to a righteous act. To perform a *mitzvah* is to carry out an act of righteousness in accordance with Jewish law. (Plural: *mitzvot*)
Ohel	A place where a person of note is buried with special honour. Similar in concept to a mausoleum, an *ohel* could be no more than a fenced-off area of the cemetery, to a special building built over the *matzevah*.
Shtetl	Small village comprising mainly Jewish inhabitants. Described as being a world within a world, Shtetl was the consummation of community, commerce, religious and family life often in rural central and eastern Europe.
Sukkah	Temporary dwelling generally made from timber and freshly cut branches and decorated with fruit. Used during the festival of *Sukkot* - tabernacles.
Tzaddik	(Lit.: 'Righteous') A righteous or esteemed pious man in the community. The term *tzaddik* was generally only applied to rabbis of particular note who were known for their wealth of wisdom or good deeds. (Plural: *tzaddikim*)
Yahrzeit	The anniversary of someone's death in the Jewish tradition.